INVESTABLE BENCHMARKS

Second Edition

A Guide to ETFs, Technology and Leverage

David S. Kreinces

INVESTABLE BENCHMARKS – SECOND EDITION

Copyright © 2021 by David Kreinces

Because of the dynamic nature of the internet, any web addresses or links contained in this book may have changed since publication and may no longer be valid. Websites were accessed between July 2019 and December 2020.

ISBN: 978-1-7363710-0-8

To my dad, Dr. Gerald Kreinces, teacher, friend, photographer, handyman, dentist, and boating captain!

Thank you for always being there for our family, for teaching me so much, and for countless great boating trips—even our first trip to Montauk when we got horribly seasick!

I am forever thankful for your endless love and support, your fearlessness, and your tireless passion for life, family, creativity, and productivity!

Montauk, NY

Acknowledgments

I thank G-d for every day, moment, and second and for our countless blessings.

Thank you to all my family, friends, clients, colleagues, service providers, industry visionaries, and inspirational leaders, all past and present, who have helped make *Investable Benchmarks* possible.

Special thanks go to: Elesia Kreinces, Gerald Kreinces, Erna Kreinces, Eva Kreitman, Julia Kreinces, Ben Kreinces, Matthew Kreinces, Rachel Stier, Marsha Birnbaum, Janet Kreinces, Melissa Kreinces, Bret Birnbaum, Lance Stier, Jonathan Schwartz, Ed Holliday, Stephen Thurer, David Horowitz, Jules Hershfeld, Tom and Cathy Hoffmann, Mike and Donna Lata, Johnny Vu, Douglas Samuelson, Ron Delegge, Stuart Rosenthal, Alex Rogow, Alex Ginzburg, Jeff Bersh, Jeremy Cohen, Walter McGuire, Robert Harteveldt, Cristian Arrieta, Ari Berman, Travis Kinworthy, Yaron Rachmany, Matthew Kaufman, Michael Covel, Bret Goldberg, Brian Riley, Martin Waschitz, Jim Carter, Eyal Yaffe, Ken Benedict, Sam Baughn, Charles Dhanraj, Steve Groschel, Ann Wigmore, Brian Clement, Dr. Leonard Coldwell, Peter Braunwart, Dennis Rivera, George Kushner, Mitch Peterson, Asaf Silberstein, Greg Reid, Clint Arthur, Alison

Savitch, Alex Mandossian, Rich Roll, Chris Carrion, Diane Naveau, Maria Moshe, Moe Lam, Chrifa Rasul, Thomesa Lydon, Bob Proctor, Ryan Long, Michelle Matich, Jill Gurr, Kimberly McKinney, Rhonda Byrne, Wallace Wattles, Hal Elrod, Erich von Daniken, Malala Yousafzai, Kip Anderson, Morgan Kehgun, Beyoncé, Tom Brady, Paul McCartney, Carl Lewis, Max Planck, and Isaac Newton.

Also, extra thanks to everyone who helped us put the book and website together including: Elizabeth (Betty) Norlin, Lawrence Ineno, Chris Gibson, Mike Dobransky, Claire Aiken, Sharón Lynn Wyeth, and Arkadi and Alexander Velitchko. Last, many thanks for the *Investable Benchmarks* covers go to Marcy Pellegrino, Ashli Shapiro, and Brandon Andre.

Table of Contents

Foreword

Jonathan Schwartz on Asset TV

Jonathan Schwartz, Partner
ETF Portfolio Management (ETF PM)

Growing up in New York, I made some great lifelong friends from the Schechter School of Long Island. After college and many years working as a trader at a large fund in Manhattan, a close friend reconnected me with David Kreinces, a third-grade classmate I remembered well.

As David and I reconnected, I learned we both traded exchange-traded funds (ETFs) with rules-based techniques. After countless conversations about trading and the future of Wall Street, I became an ETF Portfolio Management (ETF PM) client.

The firm's concept for efficient "investable benchmarks" made great sense to me. Back when I was managing 10 traders and training them on advanced techniques, I constantly reviewed a wide range of strategies. During that time, passive index investing often outperformed active traders.

When I saw that David offered clients a range of passive ETF portfolios, including the recommendation from Yale's CIO, David Swensen, I knew Kreinces was sincere and passionate about maximizing client value.

I remember in 2014 when David called me excitedly to explain his veritable epiphany for upgrading the firm's portfolios. After years of offering clients traditional, unleveraged ETF indexing, and trend following, he quickly realized that certain new leveraged ETFs could be extremely effective investment tools when used properly.

While many financial advisors strongly recommended avoiding leveraged ETFs entirely, David disagreed. Although he had never used leverage for clients in the past, the supporting data was too strong to resist.

In fact, the concept of applying leverage to a low-risk portfolio was already being employed successfully by top hedge funds, including Bridgewater and PanAgora. ETF PM just brought this advanced concept to individual investors in a simple, ultra-low-cost solution.

By 2016, David had upgraded ETF PM's passive investment solutions to use leveraged ETFs and, the following year, I decided to join the firm as a partner. While 2018 was challenging for all investors, we were pleased to see leveraged income and growth outperform strongly in 2019 and 2020.

Overall, I believe investable benchmarks are important tools for all investors, and ETF PM's versions are revolutionary in the world of money management. David presents these concepts in a fun, easy-to-read guide to help you protect and grow your financial future—and your legacy.

About Jonathan Schwartz

Jonathan Schwartz has over twenty-five years of experience in portfolio management. During most of his career, Jonathan worked as a proprietary trader. He managed a desk of 10 traders, monitored various portfolios, and implemented a sector trend following strategy focused on relative strength.

Introduction

Fig. 1: Investable Benchmarks

Name	Inception
S&P 500	1957
Nasdaq-100	1985
Nasdaq-100 3x	2010
Income & Growth 3x	2016
Income & Tech 3x	2017

Source: Wikipedia and ETF PM.

Investable benchmarks are an important starting point for all investors to see the passive index fund performance for their risk level. From the S&P 500 to efficient exchange-traded fund (ETF) portfolios, strategic index investing has delivered strong long-term returns.

Prepare for Change

The Greek philosopher Heraclitus explained that "life is flux," meaning "all things change."[1] Given this truth, the leading investable benchmark portfolios are certain to change over time. In order for you to stay current, I invite you to take a stroll down Wall Street with me, as I explain some of the most important investment trends for you and your family.

Strategic Diversification

This book combines content from ETF Portfolio Management's (ETF PM) articles and blogs, with our latest research and analysis on leading investment trends. Harry Markowitz reputedly said, "Diversification is the only free lunch," in investing and this book shows that leveraged diversification can be a free retirement nest egg.[2]

In each new edition, we plan to publish an updated version of the book with the additional performance data, along with some of our most important new research.

Chapter 1
Asset Class ETFs

Over the past few decades, investors have increasingly been using asset class exchange-traded funds (ETFs) to invest globally. In fact, BlackRock and Vanguard, the two largest ETF issuers, are also the world's largest asset managers. Warren Buffett and Yale's CIO, David Swensen, are additional examples of leading investors who strongly recommend asset class ETFs.

Types of Investments

Traditional asset class ETFs are index funds that can be traded intraday like stocks, providing efficient tools for core portfolio diversification. By using more automation, index ETFs help investors avoid many of the costs, mistakes, and tax in-efficiency associated with active management by human portfolio managers.

U.S. Stocks Outperformed

Over the past decade, these asset class ETFs (figure 2) show that U.S. stocks outperformed, while commodities, emerging markets, gold, and foreign stocks all underperformed.

Fig. 2: Asset Class ETF Performance

Asset Class ETF	9.8 Yr. Annualized	9.8 Yr. Total	Worst Year
US Stocks *(SPY)*	13%	224%	-37%
Long-Term Treasury Bonds *(TLT)*	9%	124%	-22%
Global Stocks *(VT)*	8%	113%	-42%
Real Estate *(VNQ)*	8%	110%	-37%
Foreign Stocks *(VEA)*	4%	52%	-41%
Gold *(GLD)*	3%	29%	-28%
Emerging Markets *(VWO)*	2%	25%	-53%
Commodities *(GSG)*	-11%	-68%	-47%

All data as of September 30, 2020. Worst Year is the worst calendar year since 2000. *Source*: StockCharts, Yahoo and ETF PM.

However, past performance can never guarantee future results and, since 2000, each of these asset classes had a material negative calendar year. Even protective long-term Treasury bonds were down 22 percent in 2009. In figures 3 and 4, the respective ETF details and annual returns are provided.

Fig. 3: Asset Class ETF Details

Asset Class:	US Stocks	Foreign Stocks	Emerging Markets	Global Stocks	Real Estate	Long-Term Treasuries	Commodities	Gold
Symbol	SPY	VEA	VWO	VT	VNQ	TLT	GSG	GLD
ETF Assets (billions)	$412	$77	$63	$15	$29	$20	$0.7	$78
Expense Ratio	0.10%	0.05%	0.10%	0.08%	0.12%	0.15%	0.76%	0.40%
Issuer	State Street	Vanguard	Vanguard	Vanguard	Vanguard	iShares	iShares	State Street

All data as of 10/14/20. ETF Assets are in billions of dollars. *Source:* Morningstar and ETF PM.

Fig. 4: Asset Class ETF Annual Returns

Asset Class:	US Stocks	Foreign Stocks	Emerging Markets	Global Stocks	Real Estate	Long-Term Treasuries	Commodities	Gold
Total Return	257%	52%	25%	129%	110%	124%	-68%	29%
Annualized Return	13%	4%	2%	8%	8%	9%	-11%	3%
Worst Year	-37%	-41%	-53%	-42%	-37%	-22%	-47%	-28%
Symbol	SPY	VEA	VWO	VT	VNQ	TLT	GSG	GLD
YTD 9/30/20	6%	-6%	5%	1%	-13%	22%	-34%	24%
2019	31%	23%	21%	27%	29%	14%	16%	18%
2018	-4%	-15%	-15%	-10%	-6%	-2%	-14%	-2%
2017	22%	26%	31%	24%	5%	9%	4%	11%
2016	12%	3%	12%	9%	9%	1%	10%	9%
2015	1%	-0%	-15%	-2%	2%	-2%	-34%	-12%
2014	14%	-6%	1%	4%	30%	27%	-33%	-1%
2013	32%	22%	-5%	23%	2%	-14%	-2%	-28%
2012	16%	19%	19%	17%	18%	3%	-1%	5%
2011	2%	-13%	-19%	-8%	9%	34%	-3%	11%

Performance data over 9.8 years as of 9/30/20. Past performance can never guarantee future results. Worst Year is the worst calendar year since 2000. *Source:* Morningstar and ETF PM.

Before I discuss how to combine these leading asset class ETFs into strategic portfolios, let's review wisdom from some legendary investors that will be highlighted in chapter 2.

Chapter 2
Words of Wisdom

Stephen Thurer and David Kreinces at
Bear Stearns in 1999

A few years after I graduated from Emory University, two close college friends referred me for a job working with them at Bear Stearns in Manhattan. From 1996 to 1999, I was fortunate to work on a top ranked institutional research team in Bear Stearns' high yield bond department, covering the media sector. There were many great people in that firm, including some who were very old friends.

Pay It Forward

Oren Cohen, the top-ranked research analyst who hired me, often reminded me that equity markets are efficient, and I should stick with passive index funds. He also recommended the top index investing book at the time, *A Random Walk Down Wall Street*, by Burton Malkiel.

Thankfully, both Cohen and Malkiel gave me important words of wisdom that would later shape my career as a portfolio manager.

Lessons from Legends

There are many words of wisdom that I have found helpful, and would like to pass along, including these:

1) John Maynard Keynes & Gary Shilling: *"The markets can remain irrational longer than you can remain solvent."* [3]

2) Harry Markowitz: *"Diversification is the only free lunch."* [4]

3) Nassim Taleb: *"Rare events are always unexpected, otherwise they would not occur."* [5]

Keynes & Shilling

The famed economists John Maynard Keynes and Gary Shilling are both known for explaining that *"The market can remain irrational longer than you can remain solvent."*[6]

This quote explains that financial markets will surprise most of us for extended periods. Tulip mania (1634 to 1637),[7] Japan's Nikkei 225 secular decline (1989 to 2009),[8] and the Internet Bubble (1994 to 2000)[9] are just a few well-known examples of environments that were shocking for many years.

Harry Markowitz

Nobel Prize winning economist Harry Markowitz said, *"Diversification is the only free lunch."*[10]

This quote refers to the fact that attractive long-term investments, with somewhat opposite performance rhythms, can be combined to form portfolios with better risk-adjusted returns than their components, thereby producing a free lunch.

Nassim Taleb

Nassim Taleb

Fooled by Randomness by fund manager Nassim Taleb is a personal favorite. Taleb highlights the need for investors to maintain strict risk controls for unexpected events. He said, *"Rare events are always unexpected, otherwise they would not occur."*[11]

For example, the collapse of hedge fund Long-Term Capital Management in 1998,[12] the September 11 attacks in 2001,[13] the Lehman Brothers' bankruptcy in 2008,[14] and the Coronavirus Crash in 2020, all reflect the wide range of unexpected events that can occur.

Priceless Lessons

All of the priceless lessons mentioned here highlight the need for strategic diversification. The next chapter reviews various portfolio solutions that solve this basic need with leading ETFs.

Chapter 3
Strategic Diversification

Balance

In *The Karate Kid*, karate master Mr. Miyagi teaches Daniel LaRusso the critical importance of balance in karate—and in life. I can still hear Mr. Miyagi yelling: "Balance, Daniel-san, balance!"

Balance, Daniel-san!

LaRusso needed strategic balance, discipline, and innovation to triumph, and investors need these qualities as well. Luckily, strategic portfolio balance can be accomplished with just two asset class ETFs.

Discipline and innovation are more difficult attributes that take time, research, and experience to improve. Ultimately, these dynamics are all interconnected, and the stronger your core portfolio balance, the easier it will be to maintain discipline and innovation long-term.

Types of Portfolios

Portfolio diversification comes in four main sizes, or "asset allocations," according to the respective risk and return targets:

Size or Asset Allocation	*Risk and Return Target*
1. Small	Income
2. Medium	Balanced income and growth
3. Large	Growth
4. Extra-large	Aggressive growth

Yale University, New Haven, CT

Swensen ETF Portfolio

In 2005, David Swensen, famed chief investment officer of Yale University, published *Unconventional Success*, in which he recommended a growth portfolio using low-cost index ETFs and

Treasury bonds. The Swensen ETF Portfolio is a 70/30 growth solution with an efficient multi-asset class combination of global equities, real estate, and two forms of government bonds.

Swensen's book also highlights the importance of using Treasury bonds for protection rather than a return contribution. The asset allocation includes six ETFs with 55 percent in global equities (VTI, VEA, VWO), 15 percent in real estate (VNQ), and 30 percent divided evenly between government bond ETFs (IEF and TIP).[1]

Over the past 9.8 years, Swensen's growth portfolio returned 7 percent annualized, or 102 percent in total return. However, since 2000, the worst calendar year for this portfolio was down 26 percent in 2008.

Risk Level

The problem with growth portfolios in general, including Swensen's above, is their risk level. These portfolios typically perform well in strong up markets, but a calendar year return of a 26 percent drop, or worse, is far too painful for many investors to endure.

So, how do investors reduce their portfolio risk?

Bonds

Investors typically use bonds to reduce portfolio risk and Treasuries have often been the best shock absorber when stocks crash.

Over the past 92 years, from 1928 to 2019, the S&P 500 returned 9.7 percent annualized (figures 5 and 6). However, the worst calendar years were 1931 with a decline of 44 percent and, more recently, 2008 with a drop of 37 percent.

Fig. 5: Performance over 92 Years

Performance	S&P 500	10-Yr. Treasuries	50/50 Portfolio
Annualized Return	9.7%	4.9%	7.9%
Worst Year	-44%	-11%	-23%

Performance data over 92 years from 1928 to 2019.
Source: New York University and ETF PM.

Over the same period, Intermediate-Term (10-year) Treasury Bonds delivered 4.9 percent annualized with a worst calendar year loss of 11 percent. Together, a hypothetical 50/50 portfolio of these two asset class ETFs delivered a 7.9 percent annualized return with the worst calendar years in 1931 down 23 percent and, more recently, in 2008 down 8 percent. Therefore, the equal combination of the S&P 500 and 10-year Treasury bonds delivered a better risk-adjusted return than the S&P 500 alone.

Fig. 6: Growth of $10,000 over 92 Years

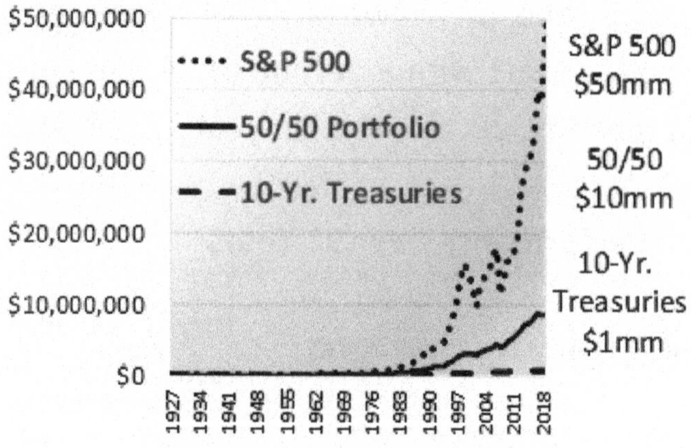

Performance data over 92 years from 1928 to 2019. mm millions. *Source*: New York University and ETF PM.

Long-Term Treasury Bonds

In recent years, the best bond ETF has been long-term Treasuries (TLT) as this core asset class has repeatedly delivered critical portfolio protection. In the 2008 financial crisis, the S&P 500 fell 37 percent while long-term Treasuries rose by 34 percent that year (figure 7), and the Aggregate Bond Index (AGG) gained just 5 percent.

In the first quarter of 2020, during the Coronavirus Crash, the S&P 500 fell by 19 percent as long-term Treasuries gained 22 percent. This level of extraordinary portfolio protection is difficult for many investors to appreciate. When bond returns were needed the most, TLT strongly outperformed other bond index ETFs.

Then again, in 2011, the European debt crisis drove TLT to another 34 percent full-year gain, even after the U.S. risk-free credit rating was downgraded for the first time in history. The Aggregate Bond Index gained just 8 percent that year.

In fact, long-term Treasuries have significantly outperformed other bond index ETFs. Over the past 9.8 years, TLT gained 9 percent annualized, or 124 percent in total return, almost three times the Aggregate Bond Index.

However, long-term Treasury bonds (TLT) still had extreme calendar year declines as well. In 2009 and 2013, TLT returned a 22 percent loss and a 14 percent decline, respectively (figure 8).

Fig. 7: Bond Index ETFs

Bond ETFs	S&P 500 Worst Years				9.8 Yr. Annualized	9.8 Yr. Total	ETF Assets
	2008	2011	2015	2018			
TIPS (TIP)	-3%	13%	-2%	-1%	4%	41%	$21b
Aggregate Bond Index (AGG)	5%	8%	0%	0%	4%	44%	$75b
Intermediate-Term Treasuries (IEF)	18%	15%	2%	1%	5%	57%	$22b
Long-Term Treasuries (TLT)	34%	34%	-2%	-2%	9%	124%	$20b
S&P 500 (SPY)	-37%	2%	1%	-4%	13%	224%	$295b

Performance data as of 9/30/20. S&P 500 Wost Years are the worst calendar years since 2003. *Source:* StockCharts, Morningstar, and ETF PM.

Fig. 8: Extreme Calendar Years

ETF	Symbol	'08	'09	'11	'13	'14	'15	'18	19	YTD '20	9.8 Yr. Annualized*
20+ Yr. Treasuries	TLT	34%	-22%	34%	-14%	27%	-2%	-2%	14%	22%	9%
S&P 500	SPY	-37%	26%	2%	32%	13%	1%	-4%	31%	6%	13%
Balanced Portfolio	Balanced	-2%	2%	18%	9%	20%	0%	-3%	23%	14%	11%

Performance data as of 9/30/20. YTD year to date. Balanced Portfolio is half TLT and half SPY. Past performance can never guarantee future results. *Source:* Morningstar and ETF PM.

Balanced Portfolio

Over the past 9.8 years, a hypothetical Balanced Portfolio, with an even combination of the S&P 500 (SPY) and long-term Treasuries (TLT), delivered a total return of 181 percent, or 11 percent annualized (figures 9 and 10).

Fig. 9: Balanced Portfolio

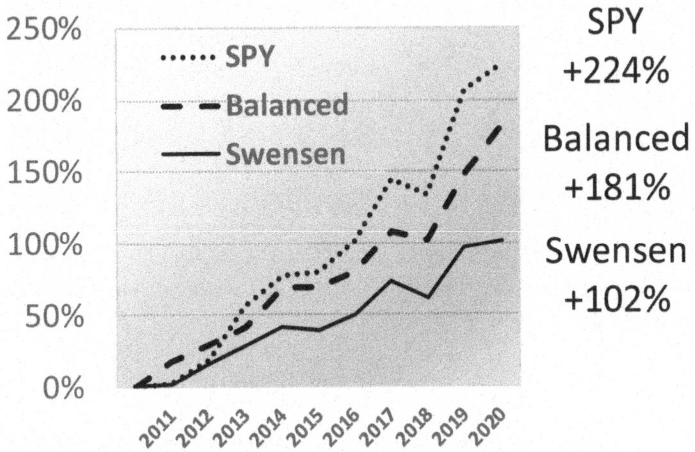

Performance data over 9.8 years as of 9/30/20.
Source: Morningstar and ETF PM.

Fig. 10: Balanced Portfolio Annual Returns

Performance	Swensen	S&P 500	Balanced Portfolio
Total Return	102%	224%	181%
Annualized Return	7%	13%	11%
Worst Year	-26%	-37%	-3%

Annual Returns	Swensen	SPY	Balanced
YTD 9/30/20	2%	6%	14%
2019	21%	31%	23%
2018	-6%	-4%	-3%
2017	15%	22%	15%
2016	8%	12%	6%
2015	-1%	1%	-0%
2014	9%	14%	20%
2013	11%	32%	9%
2012	14%	16%	10%
2011	2%	2%	18%

Performance data over 9.8 years as of 9/30/20. Worst Year is the worst calendar year since 2000. *Source:* Morningstar, StockCharts, and ETF PM.

The worst calendar year declines for this Balanced Portfolio were just a 3 percent loss in 2018 and a 2 percent decline in 2008. In fact, the 3 percent dip was far less severe than the worst year declines in the Swensen Portfolio and S&P 500 of 26 percent and 37 percent, respectively.

Prepare for Change

Historically, this balanced portfolio significantly outperformed growth investing on a risk-adjusted basis, but periods in the future may favor other asset classes, such as emerging markets. Balanced portfolios may need modification or additional risk controls at times, and investors should always be prepared to sell positions as needed.

In chapters 4 and 5, let's explore how certain indexes and balanced portfolios enable the moderate use of leverage.

Chapter 4
The Future of Investing

Recent trends suggest the future of investing may include more technology, leverage, and emerging markets. In fact, there seems to be a growing concern regarding the competitiveness of human labor versus smart machines in general.

Technology

In 2017, SoftBank CEO Masayoshi Son, one of the world's leading technology investors, raised a $100 billion Vision Fund and predicted that machine driven artificial intelligence (AI) may reach IQs of 10,000 within 30 years.[1] Note, Mensa measures human genius up to an IQ of 200.

Masayoshi Son, SoftBank CEO

SpaceX and Tesla CEO Elon Musk seems to agree as he said that "robots will do everything better than us"[2] and "AI is far more dangerous than nukes."[3]

SpaceX and Tesla CEO Elon Musk

By the second quarter of 2018, Warren Buffett got the message and admitted that he was wrong in not owning certain big technology stocks.[4] This capitulation by the world's largest fundamental investor highlights the extraordinary demand for technology in diversified investment portfolios.

The Future of Labor

Masayoshi Son and SoftBank are now working on Vision Fund 2 to further broaden their stable of AI investments.[5] Musk is also busy with a range of companies and projects revolutionizing transportation, energy, AI, and communications through semi-autonomous cars, reusable rockets, hyperloop technology and tunneling systems, batteries, solar, brain-computer interfaces (BCIs), and a megaconstellation of satellites called

Starlink. In fact, in 2019, Musk estimated that Starlink could eventually generate $30 billion in annual revenue for SpaceX.[6]

Artificial Intelligence

Advancements in technology and artificial intelligence (AI) are widely expected to deliver an era of unprecedented innovation. Recent examples include the growth in cryptocurrencies this past decade, and in June 2020, SpaceX became the first commercial aerospace company to take astronauts "off-world,"[7] in restarting the U.S. "crewed launch business."[8] Musk also predicted that AI will enable fully autonomous Tesla cars to appreciate in value materially once the company completes certain upgrades over the next few years.[9] This means that Musk and Tesla may effectively give away far more cars than Oprah!

Own the Matrix

Technology has been a leading long-term investment trend, and Forbes magazine's billionaire list is dominated by technology company founders.[10] Simply owning the technology matrix may be the best defense workers have against job loss or wage stagnation from automation. In the next chapter, dynamic ETFs are discussed that let you own the global technology complex both with or without leverage.

Chapter 5
Leveraged ETFs

Super Funds

Over the past , Wall Street created leveraged ETFs giving investors the ability to target returns up to three times the respective unleveraged index. While certain leveraged ETFs may appear to be alien 'super funds,' they are often misunderstood.

Leveraged ETFs do not work perfectly, and some may not work at all.[1] However, select leveraged asset class and sector ETFs have delivered spectacular performance.[2]

In this chapter, I will review some of the leading leveraged technology and bond ETFs, and in the following chapter, I will cover how these new investment tools can be combined within a balanced portfolio.

U Can't Touch This

Figures 11 and 12 show details on a range of select 3x leveraged ETFs. Over the past ten years, these ETFs delivered 383 percent to 4,172 percent in total return, or 18 percent to 47 percent annualized.

Fig. 11: Leveraged ETF Performance

Asset Class ETFs	Total Return	Annualized
Nasdaq-100 3x *(TQQQ)*	4,172%	47%
Technology 3x *(TECL)*	2,673%	41%
Semiconductor 3x *(SOXL)*	2,062%	37%
S&P 500 3x *(UPRO)*	905%	27%
LT Treasuries 3x *(TMF)*	383%	18%
S&P 500 (SPY)	224%	13%

All data over 9.8 years through 9/30/20. *Source*: Morningstar.com, Direxion, ProShares, and ETF PM.

When it comes to long-term ETF performance, *U Can't Touch This!* (Lyrics by MC Hammer).

MC Hammer

Fig. 12: Leveraged ETF Details

	S&P 500 3x	Nasdaq 100 3x	Semiconductor 3x	Technology 3x	Long-Term Treasuries 3x
Symbol	UPRO	TQQQ	SOXL	TECL	TMF
Expense Ratio	0.93%	0.95%	0.96%	1.08%	1.05%
ETF Assets (billions)	$1.5	$8.8	$1.5	$1.6	$0.3
Issuer	ProShares	ProShares	Direxion	Direxion	Direxion

All data as of 10/20/20. ETF Assets are in billions of dollars. *Source:* Morningstar.com, Direxion and ProShares.

Clearly, these leveraged ETFs have materially outperformed the unleveraged S&P 500 (SPY), which delivered just 224 percent in total return, or 13 percent annualized.[3] In fact, the S&P 500 3x (UPRO) returned 905 percent, roughly four times the total return of the unleveraged SPY.

Moderate Leverage

The 3x ETFs give investors 200 percent more exposure than their principal investment alone. While this may sound like an extreme amount of leverage, 200 percent is just half the leverage often used to buy a home.

When a 20 percent down payment is used to buy a house, 80 percent of the purchase price that is borrowed through a mortgage reflects 400 percent leverage (80 percent divided by 20 percent) on the investor's principal. Therefore, homebuyers often use double the leverage of 3x index ETFs.

Risk Control

In this chapter, almost 10 full calendar years of actual leveraged ETF returns are reviewed. Since the leveraged ETFs did not exist in 2008, this book reports just the respective unleveraged ETF figures for that extreme year.

Regardless, historical performance can never guarantee future results and investors should always be prepared to sell portfolio holdings to control risk as needed.

S&P 500 3x (UPRO)

The S&P 500 (SPY) is the diversified equity ETF with the most assets at $295 billion, and this large-cap index reflects roughly 80 percent of the total domestic stock market. The four largest holdings, all technology companies (Apple, Microsoft, Amazon, and Alphabet), together account for 20 percent of the index.[4]

The S&P 500 3x (UPRO, inception 2009) is a leveraged ETF that targets three times the daily return of the unleveraged S&P 500 index. Over the past 9.8 years, UPRO gained a hefty 905 percent in total return, or 27 percent annualized (figures 13 and 14).

This leveraged asset class ETF performed extremely well. Again, UPRO's total return was four times the 224 percent return of the unleveraged SPY.

Fig. 13: S&P 500 3x (UPRO) Total Return

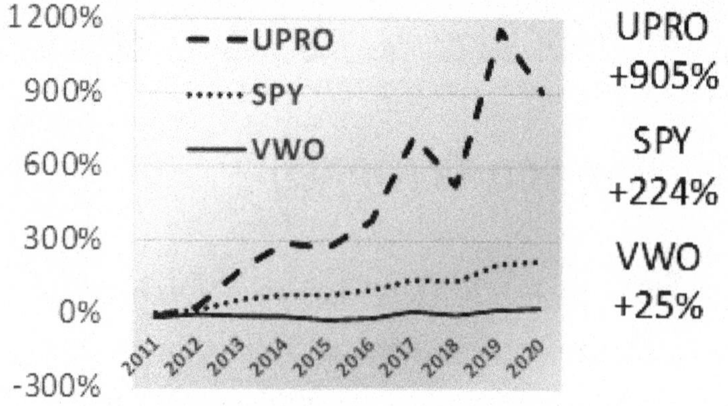

Performance data over 9.8 years as of 9/30/20.
Source: Morningstar, ProShares and ETF PM.

However, over the first nine months of 2020, the unleveraged SPY gained 6 percent while UPRO fell by 20 percent, a big disappointment for investors. In certain types of extreme volatility, such as 2020, the daily compounding of leveraged returns can produce adverse results. Investors should always gauge their exposure to leveraged ETFs very carefully.

Fig. 14: S&P 500 3x (UPRO) Annual Returns

Performance	Emerging Markets	S&P 500	S&P 500 3x
Total Return	25%	224%	905%
Annualized Return	2%	13%	27%
Worst Year	-32%	-37%	n/a
Annual Returns	**VWO**	**SPY**	**UPRO**
YTD 9/30/20	5%	6%	-20%
2019	21%	31%	102%
2018	-15%	-4%	-25%
2017	31%	22%	71%
2016	12%	12%	30%
2015	-15%	1%	-5%
2014	1%	14%	38%
2013	-5%	32%	119%
2012	19%	16%	46%
2011	-19%	2%	-11%

Performance data over 9.8 years as of 9/30/20. Worst Year is the worst calendar year since 2000. *Source*: Morningstar, ProShares and ETF PM.

Note, in the crash of 2008, the unleveraged SPY lost 37 percent, and UPRO's performance that year would have been far worse. In fact, during the

Coronavirus Crash of 2020, UPRO fell by 78 percent in just five weeks. Therefore, be sure to make any allocations to UPRO most cautiously.

Nasdaq-100 3x (TQQQ)

One of the largest equity indexes overweight in technology is the Nasdaq-100 (QQQ). This leading growth ETF is comprised of 100 of the largest non-financial companies listed on the Nasdaq. Roughly 42 percent of the Nasdaq-100 exposure is concentrated in Apple, Microsoft, Amazon, and Alphabet, more than double their exposure in the S&P 500.

In this one index, investors cover many leading technology trends such as: artificial intelligence, cloud computing, video streaming, autonomous cars, fifth-generation wireless (5G), mobile technology, computer vision, smartphones, virtual reality, Bitcoin, cryptocurrencies, and blockchain.

Over the past 9.8 years, the Nasdaq 100 3x (TQQQ, inception 2010) gained a tremendous 4,172 percent in total return, or 47 percent annualized (figures 15 and 16).

Fig. 15: Nasdaq 100 3x (TQQQ) Total Return

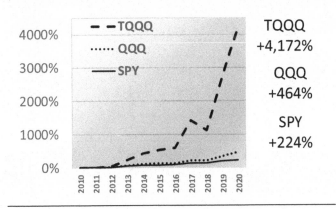

Performance data over 9.8 years as of 9/30/20.
Source: Morningstar, ProShares and ETF PM.

However, in 2018, the unleveraged QQQ was flat while TQQQ fell by 20 percent that year. Investors should gauge their exposure to TQQQ with extreme caution as well.

Fig. 16: Nasdaq 100 3x (TQQQ) Annual Returns

Performance	S&P 500	Nasdaq-100	Nasdaq-100 3x
Total Return	224%	464%	4,172%
Annualized Return	13%	19%	47%
Worst Year	-37%	-42%	n/a
Annual Returns	SPY	QQQ	TQQQ
YTD 9/30/20	6%	31%	51%
2019	31%	39%	134%
2018	-4%	-0%	-20%
2017	22%	33%	119%
2016	12%	7%	11%
2015	1%	10%	17%
2014	14%	19%	57%
2013	32%	37%	140%
2012	16%	18%	52%
2011	2%	3%	-8%

Performance data over 9.8 years as of 9/30/20. Worst Year is the worst calendar year since 2000. *Source*: Morningstar, ProShares and ETF PM.

Note, in the crash of 2008, the unleveraged Nasdaq 100 (QQQ) fell by 42 percent and TQQQ would certainly have fallen precipitously had it existed that year. In addition, during the Coronavirus Crash in 2020, TQQQ fell by 73 percent in five weeks. Investors should always engage strict risk controls when making material allocations to risk assets, especially when using leverage.

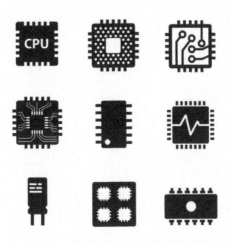

Semiconductor 3x (SOXL)

As you might expect, the Semiconductor 3x ETF (SOXL) has also been an extraordinary investment. Technology is the engine for global productivity, and semiconductors are the foundation of the technology sector.

Over the past 9.8 years, SOXL (inception 2010) gained 2,062 percent in total return, or 37 percent annualized (Figures 17 and 18).

Fig. 17: Semiconductor 3x (SOXL) Total Return

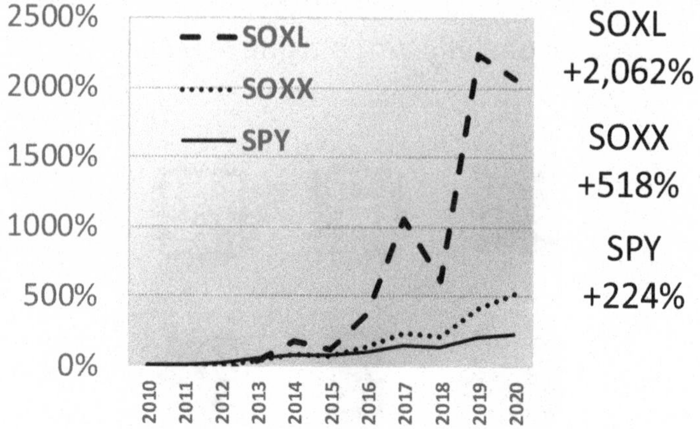

Performance data over 9.8 years as of 9/30/20.
Source: Morningstar, Direxion and ETF PM.

However, in 2018, the unleveraged SOXX lost just 6 percent while SOXL fell 39 percent, more than double the 18 percent loss expected. Clearly, SOXL may be far too volatile for many investors.

Fig. 18: Semiconductor 3x (SOXL) Annual Returns

Performance	S&P 500	SOXX	SOXL
Total Return	224%	518%	2,062%
Annualized Return	13%	21%	37%
Worst Year	-37%	-52%	n/a
Annual Returns	**SPY**	**SOXX**	**SOXL**
YTD 9/30/20	6%	22%	-8%
2019	31%	62%	232%
2018	-4%	-6%	-39%
2017	22%	40%	142%
2016	12%	38%	124%
2015	1%	-2%	-21%
2014	14%	30%	96%
2013	32%	41%	155%
2012	16%	7%	4%
2011	2%	-10%	-48%

Performance data over 9.8 years as of 9/30/20. Worst Year is the worst calendar year since 2000. *Source*: Morningstar, Direxion and ETF PM.

In fact, in the crash of 2008, the unleveraged semiconductor ETF (SOXX) fell by 52 percent, and SOXL would have been crushed had it existed. More recently, during the Coronavirus Crash in 2020, SOXL fell by 84 percent in eight weeks. Investors should certainly gauge their exposure to SOXL very carefully.

Technology 3x (TECL)

The ETFs tracking unleveraged Technology (XLK), and Technology 3x (TECL), are both con-centrated sector funds with 44 percent allocated to just Microsoft and Apple. Over the past 9.8 years, TECL (inception 2008) gained 2,673 percent in total return, or 41 percent annualized (figures 19 and 20).

Fig. 19: Technology 3x (TECL) Total Return

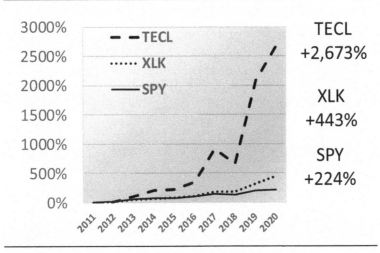

Performance data over 9.8 years as of 9/30/20.
Source: Morningstar, Direxion and ETF PM.

However, in 2018, the unleveraged XLK lost 2 percent while TECL fell by 24 percent, roughly four times the 6 percent decline expected. Since XLK fell by 42 percent in both 2000 and 2008, investors should be extremely cautious making allocations to TECL. In fact, over the three-year Internet crash from 2000 through 2002, XLK plummeted down by more than 70 percent without leverage.

Fig. 20: Technology 3x (TECL) Annual Returns

Performance	S&P 499	Technology	Technology 3x
Total Return	224%	443%	2,673%
Annualized Return	12%	16%	37%
Worst Year	-37%	-42%	n/a
Annual Returns	**SPY**	**XLK**	**TECL**
YTD 9/30/20	6%	29%	27%
2019	31%	50%	186%
2018	-4%	-2%	-24%
2017	22%	34%	125%
2016	12%	15%	37%
2015	1%	6%	5%
2014	14%	18%	52%
2013	32%	26%	88%
2012	16%	15%	33%
2011	2%	3%	-18%

Performance data over 9.8 years as of 9/30/20. Worst Year is the worst calendar year since 2000. *Source*: Morningstar, Direxion and ETF PM.

Early in 2020, during the Coronavirus Crash, TECL fell by 78 percent in just five weeks. Investors trading leveraged ETFs should always exercise extreme caution.

Long-Term Treasuries 3x (TMF)

In order to employ leverage and maintain a balanced portfolio, investors need leveraged bond ETFs as well. Over the past 9.8 years, long-term Treasuries 3x (TMF, inception 2009) delivered 383 percent in total return, almost 9 times the total return of the unleveraged Aggregate Bond Index (Figures 21 and 22).

Fig. 21: Long-Term Treasuries 3x (TMF) Total Return

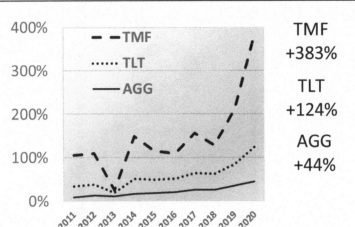

Performance data over 9.8 years as of 9/30/20.
Source: Morningstar, Direxion and ETF PM.

However, in 2013, this leveraged bond ETF crashed down 41 percent. Long-term Treasuries may also fall in sync with equities at times, as they did in 2018. Therefore, investors should always maintain additional risk controls to protect their principal as needed.

Fig. 22: LT Treasuries 3x (TMF) Annual Returns

Performance	Aggregate Bond Index	Long-term Treasuries	LT Treasuries 3x
Total Return	44%	124%	383%
Annualized Return	4%	9%	18%
Worst Year	-2%	-22%	n/a
Annual Returns	**AGG**	**TLT**	**TMF**
YTD 9/30/20	7%	22%	55%
2019	8%	14%	36%
2018	0%	-2%	-11%
2017	4%	9%	23%
2016	3%	1%	-3%
2015	1%	-2%	-14%
2014	6%	27%	101%
2013	-2%	-14%	-41%
2012	4%	3%	1%
2011	8%	34%	105%

Performance data over 9.8 years as of 9/30/20. Worst Year is the worst calendar year since 2000. *Source*: Morningstar, Direxion and ETF PM.

Extreme Caution

While certain leveraged ETFs have per-formed spectacularly well, they do not always work as expected. The daily compounding of these products can distort the full-year returns, so lever-aged ETFs often deviate materially from the target multiple of their underlying index. It is wise to be extremely cautious in using these volatile funds.

U Really Can't Touch This

In fact, many financial advisors recommend avoiding leveraged ETFs entirely or using them only for short-term trading. Vanguard even banned the purchase of leveraged ETFs in its client accounts.[5]

At some investment firms, *"u really can't touch this!"*

When discussing leveraged ETFs, I am refer-ring only to select leading asset class and sector funds. Many other leveraged ETFs that target smaller and more volatile sectors, or inverse indexes, may be far more challenging tools for in-vestors to engage.

Baby Steps

Financial conditions can change instantly. Investors should engage leveraged ETFs only with the appropriate level of balance and risk control. Even with these safeguards in place, go slowly.

Investors can use 3x ETFs in stages to target just 10 percent to 30 percent of additional exposure. It is very helpful to increase leverage in baby steps, and only after material gains accrue, in order to build a cushion for the extra risk and volatility that often comes with using leverage.

Shanghai, China

Emerging Markets

In addition to the risks associated with using leverage in general, and the risk inherent in the mechanics of leveraged ETFs, there is another important risk to monitor. The outperformance of US stocks over emerging markets this past decade may leave many investors unbalanced. If China or the emerging markets index begins to materially out-perform in the future, many investors may need to rebalance and increase their exposure to emerging markets.[6]

Prepare for Change

Remember that leveraged ETFs do not always deliver the full-year target return multiple expected, they can be extremely volatile at times, and certain global rebalancing may be needed in the future. Investors should always be prepared to sell positions and control portfolio risk.

In the next chapter, I will review balanced income and growth portfolio combinations that use leveraged ETFs strategically.

Chapter 6
Leveraged Income and Growth

Clone Your Portfolio

Would you clone your annual income if you could? How about your investment portfolio? Is your portfolio too volatile to be cloned?

Clone a Safer Portfolio

In this past decade, new leveraged ETFs enabled you to somewhat clone your investment portfolio. While it may sound wildly futuristic, this extraordinary opportunity is worth considering with the right risk controls.

When you contemplate leverage on a typical growth portfolio, the risk level would be far too dangerous for most investors. However, if you monitor the effect of moderate leverage on a strategically balanced portfolio, you may feel much differently. In addition, many investors may need to clone their investment income and growth in order to replace labor income lost to automation.[1]

Risk Parity

At ETF PM, our research indicates that a low-risk balanced portfolio is capable of generating more return, per unit of risk, than a traditional growth portfolio. In fact, one of the most effective strategies on Wall Street this past decade was "risk parity," which is also referred to as "leveraged income and growth."[2]

Risk parity refers to broadly diversified and balanced portfolios that sometimes utilize lever-age. Just imagine your retirement nest egg as a power boat.

Do you want one big risky engine or three smaller and safer engines?

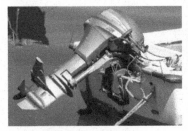

Single-Engine   *Triple-Engine*

The large single engine ("growth portfolio") has strong power but it comes with significant breakdown risk. Instead, the historical returns favor having three medium size engines ("strategic income and growth portfolios") that can collectively deliver far greater power with much lower breakdown risk.

Hedge Funds

Ray Dalio is the founder and chief investment officer of Bridgewater Associates, the world's largest hedge fund with over $100 billion under management. Bridgewater employs leveraged risk parity in its All Weather portfolio, and in recent years, leveraged risk parity has taken Wall Street by storm.[3] It seems many investors have learned that long-term Treasuries and leverage are both important tools to enhance investment performance.

Investable Benchmark Upgrade

By 2014, many of the leveraged asset class ETFs had reached their three-year point, enabling researchers to analyze these new instruments in different environments. Just two years later, in 2016, ETF PM upgraded the investable benchmarks to include an efficient range of leveraged income and growth portfolios.

Balanced 3x Portfolio

The balanced combination of the S&P 500 3x (UPRO) and long-term Treasuries 3x (TMF) is another efficient investable benchmark that investors should monitor. Over the past 9.8 years through September 2020, this Balanced 3x portfolio delivered 961 percent in total return, or 27 percent annualized (figures 22 and 23).

I estimate the worst calendar year for Balanced 3x was 2018 with a decline of 18 percent. In that year, the unleveraged Balanced Portfolio fell by just 3 percent while Balanced 3x lost double the 9 percent expected.

Fig. 23: Balanced 3x Total Return

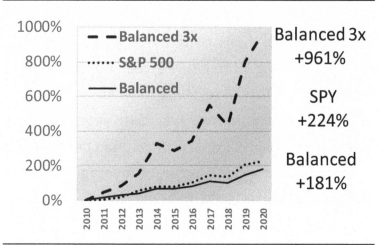

Hypothetical backtested performance data over 9.8 years as of 9/30/20. Balanced is half S&P 500 and half LT Treasury bonds. *Source*: Morningstar and ETF PM.

Back in the crash of 2008, the unleveraged Balanced Portfolio lost 2 percent, and the Balanced 3x ETFs did not exist. Regardless, investors should always be prepared to engage active risk controls as needed, especially when using leverage.

Fig. 24: Balanced 3x Annual Returns

Performance	Balanced Portfolio	S&P 500	Balanced 3x
Total Return	181%	224%	961%
Annualized Return	10%	12%	25%
Worst Year	-3%	-37%	-18%

Annual Returns	Balanced	SPY	Balanced 3x
YTD 9/30/20	14%	6%	18%
2019	23%	31%	69%
2018	-3%	-4%	-18%
2017	15%	22%	47%
2016	6%	12%	14%
2015	-0%	1%	-9%
2014	20%	14%	69%
2013	9%	32%	39%
2012	10%	16%	24%
2011	18%	2%	47%

Hypothetical backtested performance data over 9.8 years as of 9/30/20. Worst Year is the worst calendar year since 2000. *Source*: Morningstar and ETF PM.

Greatest Mathematical Discovery

The process of earning a return on accumulated gains, called "compounding," allows assets to grow exponentially larger with higher annualized return rates or longer time periods. Some believe Albert Einstein may have called compound interest the eighth wonder of the world and the greatest mathematical discovery of all time.

Albert Einstein

For example, as discussed in chapter 5, over the past 9.8 years, the S&P 500 3x (UPRO) returned 905 percent, 4 times the 224 percent total return of the unleveraged SPY (figure 11). Therefore, our research concludes that investors may benefit greatly from using select leveraged ETFs at times, albeit in a somewhat slow, cautious, and balanced manner.

Chapter 7
Warren Buffett

Oracle of Omaha

In late 2017, Warren Buffett, one of the world's most successful investors, was about to win his 10-year bet against hedge funds.[1] At that time, I proposed that Buffett's next bet should be against leveraged income and growth.[2] The ETF portfolio that Buffett recommended is simply 90 percent S&P 500 and 10 percent cash.[3]

I made this suggestion because the data indicated that three low-risk income and growth portfolios were far more valuable than one un-leveraged growth solution. If Buffett would take this bet, it would help to highlight the extraordinary opportunity for small investors in leveraged income and growth strategies.

Extraordinary Opportunity

Over the past 9.8 years, Balanced 3x gained 961 percent, almost 5 times the 193 percent return from Buffett's portfolio (figures 25 and 26). Note, if you ever experience such extreme outperformance in the future, you may start dancing like MC Hammer!

Fig. 25: Buffett ETF Portfolio Total Return

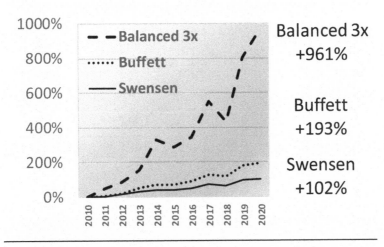

Hypothetical backtested performance data over 9.8 years as of 9/30/20. *Source*: Morningstar and ETF PM.

Balanced 3x outperformed Buffett's ETF portfolio by a large margin in seven of the ten periods, including a massive gain of 69 percent in 2014 and again in 2019. During the first three quarters of 2020, Balanced 3x outperformed once again with a gain of 18 percent versus 5 percent for Buffett.

Fig. 26: Buffett ETF Portfolio Annual Returns

Performance	Swensen	Buffett	Balanced 3x
Total Return	102%	193%	961%
Annualized Return	7%	12%	27%
Worst Year	-26%	-33%	-18%

Annual Returns	Swensen	Buffett	Balanced 3x
YTD 9/30/20	2%	5%	18%
2019	21%	28%	69%
2018	-6%	-4%	-18%
2017	15%	20%	47%
2016	8%	11%	14%
2015	-1%	1%	-9%
2014	9%	12%	69%
2013	11%	29%	39%
2012	14%	14%	24%
2011	2%	2%	47%

Hypothetical backtested performance data over 9.8 years as of 9/30/20. Worst Year is the worst calendar year since 2000. *Source*: Morningstar and ETF PM.

Risk Level

Leveraged income and growth also delivered lower risk. Since 2000, the worst calendar year for Buffett's aggressive growth portfolio was 2008 with a decline of 33 percent. The unleveraged Balanced Portfolio lost just 2 percent that year, and the Balanced 3x ETFs did not exist. However, in 2018, the unleveraged Balanced Portfolio fell by 3 percent, and the Balanced 3x fell by 18 percent.

That Was Easy

Balanced 3x trounced Buffett's ETF portfolio, and it only underperformed in two of the ten periods. Clearly, leveraged ETFs may enhance performance exponentially and cloning a safer portfolio could deliver extraordinary results at times.

Chapter 8
Bogle's Folly

In 2019, John "Jack" Bogle, Vanguard's acclaimed founder, died at age 89. He will always be remembered for pioneering index funds that materially enhanced value for the average investor. Thanks to Bogle, the S&P 500 index has been the world's top aggressive growth investable benchmark for decades with indexed assets comprising over $3 trillion.[1]

Bogle's Folly

The S&P 500 index fund that Bogle launched in 1976, called "First Index Investment Trust," was also known as "Bogle's Folly." Jack was ridiculed at first, but he proved his critics wrong. In fact, Bogle's Folly actually helped the S&P 500 become the world's leading investable benchmark, a critical innovation and starting point for all investors.[2]

Investable Benchmarks

I was inspired by Bogle and Vanguard early in my career. Thus, today I often explain that our company, ETF PM, is building a "next-generation" Vanguard.

ETF PM's investable benchmarks were mostly influenced by Jack Bogle's efficient indexing approach at Vanguard, David Swensen's diversification in *Unconventional Success*, and Ray Dalio's application of leveraged risk parity at Bridgewater.

Regardless, no matter who takes the investable benchmark torch from Jack, Bogle will always be remembered for his revolutionary vision, legendary passion, and extraordinary success in maximizing investor value.

Remembering Jack

Pensions & Investments (P&I), a widely followed institutional investor news service, published 'Remembering Jack' in January 2019 (see ETF PM news).[3]

'Remembering Jack' is a beautiful tribute to the legendary Jack Bogle by investment industry leaders. ETF PM is incredibly honored and thankful for being included, especially in remembering such an icon as Bogle.

P&I recognized ETF PM as an industry leader because of the revolutionary innovation ETF Portfolio Management shows investors at InvestableBenchmarks.com, as our company works to take the investable benchmark torch from Jack Bogle.

Follow the Math

History shows that investors should expect constant change and be prepared to adapt. While many folks resist innovation initially, as per Bogle's Folly, leading investment strategies will still evolve over time. The extraordinary success of the S&P

500 index fund and index investing in general suggest that investors do follow the math eventually.

Finance Progresses

To paraphrase the Nobel Prize-winning physicist Max Planck, science progresses one funeral at a time.[4] This means that shocking new truths are resisted, and instead of converting people, new ideas take hold in future generations. As for investing, it seems that finance progresses one index at a time. The top equity index has evolved from the Dow 30 (DIA) to the S&P 500 (SPY) and more recently to the Nasdaq-100 (QQQ) and the Nasdaq-100 3x (TQQQ).[5]

Chapter 9
Lower Your Taxes

Leveraged asset class ETFs are like multitools with a wide range of uses. In addition to upgrading your portfolio's target performance and risk control, these dynamic funds are helpful in tax planning and cash management.

Retirement Accounts

Ask your CPA or tax preparer about the annual contributions you can make to the proper retirement accounts for your situation. Try to maximize your annual deposits and consider strategies that help lower your taxes.

For example, leveraged ETFs enable investors to increase their assets invested within tax-deferred or tax-free accounts, including Roth IRAs and Education Savings Accounts. When this is done, while reducing assets invested in taxable accounts by a similar amount, investors can target greater household tax efficiency.

IRAs and 401(k) Rollovers

If your retirement account investment options do not allow for a wide range of ETF positions, consider alternative types of retirement accounts. In many cases, this means transferring 401(k) or retirement plan assets into a Rollover IRA account, also known as a "401(k) rollover" or an "IRA rollover."

Cash Management

Investors often keep cash reserves in their taxable accounts for living expenses and an emergency reserve. To enhance performance, many investors could use leveraged ETFs to increase their exposure in tax deferred accounts by a similar amount. This approach enables investors to simulate having their cash reserve funds  working long-term in their tax deferred account(s).

Index ETFs

The automation within asset class index ETFs often produces superior performance with lower expenses, less turnover, and greater tax efficiency than active management. Together, these qualities make index ETFs attractive for a wide range of strategies, including passive buy-and-hold investing.

Step-Up Basis

When long-term investment assets are inherited, the beneficiary receives the assets with a step-up basis. This means the capital gains tax on the original owner's appreciation is avoided. However, investors often need innovative portfolio solutions in order to buy-and-hold long-term and effectively invest tax-free.

Tax-Free Investing

Index funds are ideal for the step-up basis strategy. In addition to having tax efficient operations, index ETFs often deliver strong relative performance because they automatically adjust their exposure to new industry leaders over time. This means that equity ETFs protect investors from the risk of missing the next Apple or Amazon.

Still, buy-and-hold index investing requires experience, discipline, and strategic diversification to maximize decades of potential tax savings. Be sure to monitor the investable benchmark port-folios and consider an allocation to strategically balanced asset class ETFs that you can hold long-term.

Chapter 10
Prepare for Change

Johnny Mathis with Elesia and David Kreinces

Many successful celebrities and entrepre-neurs often say they must adapt to succeed. In fact, Charles Darwin helped us learn that it is not the strongest or most intelligent that survive, but those most willing to adapt.[1]

Martha Stewart and David Kreinces
at Carnegie Hall

People that understand this reality monitor a range of investable benchmarks and update their core portfolios in baby steps.

The Bottom Line

There are many uses for the top leveraged ETFs including performance enhancement, tax efficiency, cash management, and risk control. As machines ascend to thousands of IQ points, people

may actually need to clone their investment income to replace labor income.

Coco, David Kreinces, and Ice-T in New York City

While change is constant, the decade ahead
may continue to favor ETFs, technology, and leverage. Just remember Jack Bogle's Folly and follow
the math.

David Kreinces and Suzanne Somers at
Harvard Club of Boston

Stay focused on the investable benchmark portfolio appropriate for your situation, especially a version that you can hold long-term, and consider extra risk controls or rebalancing as needed. Past performance can never guarantee future results, but diversification is a free lunch, and leveraged diversification can be a free retirement nest egg.[2]

Chapter 11
The American Dream ETF

Give someone lunch and feed them for a day; teach them to invest and feed them for a lifetime! To help raise awareness for this priceless lesson, and the opportunity in leveraged diversification, I named the Nasdaq-100 3x (TQQQ) the 'American Dream ETF,' and the 'Michael Jordan of ETFs!' In an epic June 2020 YouTube webisode, ***ETF Battles: TQQQ vs. FNGU***, I added that FANG 3x (FNGU) is the 'LeBron James of ETFs,' as both have delivered legendary performance.[1]

Michael "Air" Jordan

THE GOAT ETF

In 2020, the unleveraged Nasaq-100 became just the fourth ETF to surpass $100 billion in assets, confirming market acceptance of this top growth index. Here are the other main reasons why I believe **TQQQ is the GOATE—the greatest of all-time ETF!**

1) The broadly diversified Nasdaq-100 index appears to be the next-generation S&P 500. The two indexes have the same top five holdings, and the Nasdaq-100 has double the overall technology exposure,

with earlier access to hypergrowth companies in Tesla (TSLA) and Amazon (AMZN).

2) This past decade, the Nasdaq-100 delivered more than double the S&P 500 return, and the trends in machine learning suggest technology will be far more powerful in the future.

3) Leveraged diversification can deliver a carton of extra retirement nest eggs at times.

Legendary Performance

Over the past 9.8 years, TQQQ returned almost 42x your money, or 47 percent annualized. This means that a $15,000 investment would have gained over $1 million in just 10 years. At this rate of return, just a $500 investment could reach $2 million in 21 years.

Even if TQQQ's growth rate gets cut in half for some reason, a 23 percent annualized return could still grow a $500 seed investment into $2 million in 39 years. Perhaps each person should own the technology matrix and have geniuses like Elon Musk and Jeff Bezos working for them as much as possible.

Unprecedented Innovation

In fact, unprecedented advancements in technology and cryptocurrencies give investors spectacular new growth opportunities. Over the past 10.5 years since TQQQ's inception ($1.73/share on 2/11/10), this sensational diversified ETF delivered a peak total return just over 100 times ($174.53/share on 9/2/20).

As if leveraged asset class ETFs weren't exciting enough, Bitcoin, the world's top crypto-currency and blockchain application, has actually outperformed the GOATE—TQQQ![2] Still, patiently holding even the best investments can be challenging at times and taking advantage of these leading investment trends may require an open mind and certain optimism about your future.

Frequency

Oprah

Einstein explained that "everything in life is vibration," and both Jordan and Oprah remind you to visualize your success to succeed. It seems that when accomplishing your favorite dreams in life, it is important to first envision achieving them well in order to set the appropriate mental frequency. Therefore, whenever you think about investing, or your future in general, be confident that you will make good decisions, and that you will always be happy, healthy, wealthy, and wise.

Law of Attraction

At ETF PM, our research indicates that you get what you think, so mind your thoughts and words very carefully. If you want to maximize your success, always be positive, help others as much as possible, and think and say only what you really desire. To better understand these critical concepts, study the following Law of Attraction resources.

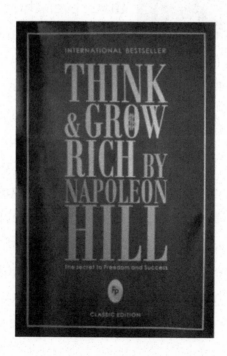

Law of Attraction Resources

1) YouTube Video: *"Think and Grow Rich,"* by Napoleon Hill, summarized by Mani Vaya
2) Netflix Movie: *The Secret* by Rhonda Byrne
3) Netflix Movie: *Heal* by Kelly Noonan
4) *The Science of Getting Rich: Financial Success Through Creative Thought* (Barnes & Noble Library of Essential Reading Null Edition) by Wallace D. Wattles.

5) YouTube Video: *"The 11 Forgotten Laws,"* explained by Bob Proctor.

Gifts That Keep Giving

In order to give back to our community, ETF Portfolio Management (ETF PM) awards Investable Benchmark Grants to hard working students in need. On an annual basis, we give grants of $500 each, in which we ask the students to invest these funds in the Nasdaq-100 3x (TQQQ), with any excess capital used to purchase shares in the Crypto Index (BITW) or Bitcoin Trust (GBTC).

Te'yanah O.   **Jericho C.**

Our intention is for these investment grants to help support financial literacy and raise awareness for the incredible opportunity in lever-aged diversification. Ultimately, we believe these critical lessons may assist countless people in maximizing their financial future and achieving their individual dreams.

Happy investing! And remember, keep your assets working while you enjoy the show!

Podcast & Market Updates

Visit ETFPM.com and subscribe separately to the ***Investable Benchmark Update (IBU)*** podcast, and our monthly performance email.

Amazon Review

Please also give us your ***Investable Benchmarks*** book review on Amazon if possible. Your review helps Amazon promote our book.

Thank you!

Disclosures

Investable Benchmarks was written to explain leading investment trends in a quick, entertaining, and easy to follow manner that may help to educate and protect the greatest number of people. The Balanced Portfolio and Balanced 3x Portfolio are similar to ETF Portfolio Management's investable benchmark portfolios. The celebrity pictures are included to make the book more enjoyable and do not imply that these celebrities are ETF PM clients. See www.ETFPM.com for full disclosures.

The performance data in this book is summary in nature for informational purposes and this book is not an offering of securities. Forward-looking statements are not a guarantee of future performance, and future events and results may differ from those anticipated.

Many of the hypothetical core models shown are similar to strategies that David Kreinces first backtested in 2016. These portfolios do not take into account an individual's investment objectives and financial circumstances. Consult your investment adviser before investing.

Performance Estimates

The performance estimates for multi-ETF portfolios herein reflect performance that would have been achieved by a hypothetical account with annual rebalancing of the respective holdings. The performance estimates are backtested and have not been audited. The performance estimates do not reflect trading fees associated with annual rebalancing and assume reinvestment of dividends.

The performance estimates also exclude any advisory fees, commissions and other transaction charges, as well as any charges relating to the custody of securities in such accounts.

Backtesting involves simulation of a quantitative investment model by applying all rules, thresholds, and strategies to a hypothetical portfolio during a specific time period. The multi-ETF portfolio performance estimates herein do not reflect the returns of actual client accounts. Backtested performance does not represent actual trading and does not reflect the impact that material market factors might have had on investor decision-making.

Remember, historical performance estimates are not indicative of future performance. The investment return and principal value of an investment in these solutions will fluctuate and may be worth more or less than the original cost when liquidated. The investment environment and market conditions may be markedly different in the future and investment returns will fluctuate in value.

These investable benchmark solutions are presented, with a view towards strategic, low-cost diversification across multiple asset classes. The performance estimates presented are for comparison purposes only. All of the information in this report was taken from sources which I believe to be reliable, yet I cannot guarantee perfect accuracy.

Leveraged ETFs

Leveraged ETFs do not deliver their exact multiple of the underlying index. On a regular basis, leveraged ETF returns may deviate materially from the underlying index multiple they target. Investors should not use leveraged ETFs without careful consideration, an appropriate asset allocation, extensive experience, and a disciplined risk-control framework.

When discussing leveraged ETFs in this book, I am referring only to leading asset class ETFs and select sectors. Smaller and more volatile sector and inverse leveraged ETFs are far more challenging tools to engage.

Individual investors should not use any investment tools without the necessary caution and experience for their risk profile.

S&P 500

SPY is an ETF for the S&P 500 Index. The S&P 500 Index is an unmanaged index of common stocks that represents the U.S. stock market. The index is mainly comprised of large cap companies and reflects roughly 80 percent of the total domestic stock market value. UPRO is an ETF that targets the S&P 500 3x.

Treasury Bonds

TLT is an ETF for 20+ Year Treasury Bonds. TMF targets this asset class 3x.

Notes

Chapter 2

1 Heraclitus

Joshua J. Mark, "Heraclitus: Life is Flux," *Ancient History Encyclopedia*, January 18, 2012. www.ancient.eu/article/75/heraclitus-life-is-flux

2 Markowitz

"The Importance of Diversification," *Barron's*, March 16, 2019. www.barrons.com/articles/the-importance-of-diversification-51552738215

3 Keynes & Shilling

"The Market Can Remain Irrational Longer Than You Can Remain Solvent," *Quote Investigator*, August 9, 2011.

www.quoteinvestigator.com/2011/08/09/remain-solvent/

4 Markowitz

"The Importance of Diversification," *Barron's*, March 16, 2019. www.barrons.com/articles/the-importance-of-diversification-51552738215

5 Taleb

Nassim Nicholas Taleb, *"Fooled by Randomness: The Hidden Role of Chance in Life and in the Markets,"* New York: Random House, 2004.

6 Keynes & Shilling

"The Market Can Remain Irrational Longer Than You Can Remain Solvent," *Quote Investigator*, August 9, 2011.

www.quoteinvestigator.com/2011/08/09/remain-solvent/

7 Tulip

Adam Hayes, "Dutch Tulip Bulb Market Bubble Definition," *Investopedia*, June 25, 2019. www.investopedia.com/terms/d/dutch_tulip_bulb_market_bubble.asp

8 Japan

Masayuki Tamura, "30 Years Since Japan's Stock Market Peaked, Climb Back Continues," *Nikkei Asian Review*, December 29, 2019. https://asia.nikkei.com/Spotlight/Datawatch/30-years-since-Japan-s-stock-market-peaked-climb-back-continues

9 **Internet**

Adam Hayes, "Dotcom Bubble," *Investopedia*, June 25, 2019. Retrieved from: https://www.investopedia.com/terms/d/dotcom-bubble.asp

10 **Markowitz**

"The Importance of Diversification," *Barron's*, March 16, 2019.
www.barrons.com/articles/the-importance-of-diversification-51552738215

11 **Taleb**

Nassim Nicholas Taleb, *"Fooled by Randomness: The Hidden Role of Chance in Life and in the Markets,"* New York: Random House, 2004.

12 **LTCM**

Roger Lowenstein, *"When Genius Failed: The Rise and Fall of Long-Term Capital Management,"* New York, Random House and Toronto: Random House of Canada Limited, 2001.

13 September 11

Marc Davis, "How September 11 Effected the U.S. Stock Market," *Investopedia*, September 11, 2017.
www.investopedia.com/financial-edge/0911/how-september-11-affected-the-u.s.-stock-market.aspx

14 Lehman

Anne Sraders, "The Lehman Brothers Collapse and How It Changed the Economy Today," *The Street*, September 12, 2018.
www.thestreet.com/markets/lehman-brothers-collapse-14703153

Chapter 3

1 Swensen

David F. Swensen, *"Unconventional Success: A Fundamental Approach to Personal Investment,"* New York: Free Press: A Division of Simon & Schuster, Inc., 2005.
www.amazon.com/Unconventional-Success-Fundamental-Approach-Investment/dp/0743228383]

Chapter 4

1 Masayoshi Son

Anita Balakrishnan, "SoftBank's Masayoshi Son Aims to Control 90 Percent of the Chip Market," *CNBC*, October 25, 2017.
www.cnbc.com/2017/10/25/softbanks-masayoshi-son-talks-ai-and-investment-on-saudi-panel.html

2 Musk

Catherine Clifford, "Elon Musk: Robots Will Be Able to Do Everything Better Than Us, " *CNBC*, July 17, 2017.
www.cnbc.com/2017/07/17/elon-musk-robots-will-be-able-to-do-everything-better-than-us.html

3 Musk

Catherine Clifford, "Elon Musk: 'Mark My Words — A.I. is Far More Dangerous Than Nukes,'" *CNBC*, March 13, 2018.
www.cnbc.com/2018/03/13/elon-musk-at-sxsw-a-i-is-more-dangerous-than-nuclear-weapons.html

4 **Warren Buffett**

Tae Kim, "Warren Buffett: I Was Wrong on Google and Amazon, Jeff Bezos Achieved a Business 'Miracle'," *CNBC,* May 7, 2018.
https://www.cnbc.com/2018/05/05/buffett-i-was-wrong-on-google-and-amazon-bezos-achieved-a-business-miracle.html

5 **Vision Fund 2**

Laurie Clarke, "SoftBank's $108 Billion Vision Fund 2 is on Shaky Ground," *Wired*, January 16, 2020.
www.wired.co.uk/article/softbank-vision-fund-2

6 **Starlink**

Michael Sheetz and Magdalena Petrova, "Why in the Next Decade Companies Will Launch Thousands More Satellites Than in All of History," *CNBC*, December 17, 2019.
www.cnbc.com/2019/12/14/spacex-oneweb-and-amazon-to-launch-thousands-more-satellites-in-2020s.html

7 **Off World**

"The Morning After: SpaceX Makes History," *Engadget*, June 1, 2020.
www.engadget.com/the-morning-after-spacex-nasa-iss-113022064.html

8 Crewed Launch

Steve Dent, "Space X's Pioneering Astronauts Board the International Space Station," *Engadget,* June 1, 2020.
www.engadget.com/spacex-crew-dragon-astronauts-board-iss-082743475.html

9 Tesla

Fred Lambert, "Elon Musk: Tesla Cars Should be Worth $100k to $200k with Full Self-Driving Package," *Electrek*, July 16, 2019.
www.electrek.co/2019/07/16/tesla-cars-worth-100k-200k-full-self-driving-package-elon-musk/

10 Forbes

Jack Schofield, "Tech Founders Dominate Forbes Magazine's Billionaire List," *ZDNet*, October 17, 2017.
www.zdnet.com/article/tech-founders-dominate-forbes-magazines-billionaire-list/

Chapter 5

1 Investments

Howard Gold, "Leveraged ETFs are the Worst Investment Ever," *MarketWatch*, October 28, 2011.
www.marketwatch.com/story/leveraged-etfs-are-the-worst-investment-ever-2011-10-28

2 **Investments**

Sweta Killa, "Bet on the Top Leveraged ETFs of the Longest-Ever Bull Market," *Nasdaq*, August 23, 2018.

www.nasdaq.com/articles/bet-top-leveraged-etfs-longest-ever-bull-market-2018-08-23

3 **SPY**

Mark Krantz, "Is SPY Stock a Buy Right Now? What to Know About World's Top Index," *Investor's Business Daily*, December 5, 2019.

www.investors.com/news/spy-stock-buy-now/

4 **Proshares Ultrapro S&P 500®**

UPRO holdings 9/30/20

www.proshares.com/media/fact_sheet/ProShares FactSheetUPRO.pdf

5 **Vanguard**

Bradley Keoun, "Triple-X ETFs Now Taboo at Vanguard as Regulators Look the Other Way," *The Street*, January 10, 2019.

www.thestreet.com/markets/triple-x-etfs-now-taboo-at-vanguard-as-regulators-look-other-way-14830195

6 China

"MSCI Completes Rebalancing of China A-Shares in Indexes," *FINEWS.ASIA*, November 28, 2019.
www.finews.asia/finance/30352-msci-completes-rebalancing-of-china-a-shares-in-indexes

Chapter 6

1 Automation

CGP Grey, "Humans Need Not Apply," August 13, 2014.
www.youtube.com/watch?v=7Pq-S557XQU

2 Risk Parity

Simon Constable, "How Trillions in Risk-Parity/Volatility Trades Could Sink the Market," *Forbes*, February 13, 2018.
www.forbes.com/sites/simonconstable/2018/02/13/how-trillions-in-risk-parityvolatility-trades-could-sink-the-market/#5c3d55402e2f

3 Dalio

Jen Wieczner, "Ray Dalio's McDonald's-Inspired Hedge Fund is Crushing His Flagship Fund," *Fortune*, July 7, 2016.
www.fortune.com/2016/07/07/bridgewater-hedge-fund-ray-dalio/

Chapter 7

1 Buffett

Mark Hulbert, "Opinion: Check Out This $1 Million Bet Warren Buffett Looks About to Win," *MarketWatch*, September 2, 2017.
www.marketwatch.com/story/check-out-this-1-million-bet-warren-buffett-looks-about-to-win-2017-09-01

2 Buffett

David Kreinces, "Next Bet for Buffett," ETF PM, September 2017.
www.etfpm.com/next-bet-warren-buffett-917/

3 Buffett

John Wasik, "COLUMN-How You Can Build on Warren Buffett's Investment Advice," *Reuters*, March 10, 2014.
www.reuters.com/article/column-wasik-buffett/column-how-you-can-build-on-warren-buffetts-investment-advice-idUSL2N0M711E20140310

Chapter 8

1 S&P 500

www.spglobal.com/spdji/en/indices/equity/sp-500/#overview

Notes

2 Bogle's Folly

Michael J. Clowes, "Importance of 'Bogle's Folly,'" *Pensions & Investments*, June 11, 2001. www.pionline.com/article/20010611/PRINT/1061 10706/importance-of-bogle-s-folly

3 Remembering Jack (Jan. 21, 2019)

www.pionline.com/article/20190121/PRINT /190129992/remembering-jack https://etfpm.com/american-dream-etf-6-20/

4 Finance Progresses

Max Planck, *Scientific Autobiography and Other Papers (New York NY: Philosophical Library, 1950)), pp. 33..* https://en.wikipedia.org/wiki/Planck%27s_princip le
Actual quote: "A new scientific truth does not triumph by convincing its opponents and making them see the light, but rather because its opponents eventually die, and a new generation grows up that is familiar with it."

5 American Dream ETF

David Kreinces, ETF Portfolio Management, LLC, "American Dream ETF," June 1, 2020. https://etfpm.com/american-dream-etf-6-20/

Chapter 10

1 Darwin
"It Is Not the Strongest of the Species That Survives But the Most Adaptable," May 4, 2014.
www.quoteinvestigator.com/2014/05/04/adapt/

2 Markowitz
"The Importance of Diversification," *Barron's*, March 16, 2019.
www.barrons.com/articles/the-importance-of-diversification-51552738215

Chapter 11

1 TQQQ vs. FNGU
ETF Portfolio Management, LLC, "ETF Battles: TQQQ vs. FNGU," June 2020.
https://etfpm.com/etf-battles-tqqq-vs-fngu-6-20/

2 Bitcoin
ETFGuide, "ETF Battles: GBTC vs. TIP – Bitcoin against TIPS, Which is the Better Inflation Hedge?," November 6, 2020.
https://www.youtube.com/watch?v=9-ag68m5vkc

Images

Chapter 3; Balance

Adler, Burke, "Balance and Success: *Inspired by the Karate Kid—We Learned the Importance of Balance in Life."*
https://www.burkealder.com/adventure/karate-kid-balance-and-success

Many image(s) used under license from Shutterstock.com.

Index

Index

Index

September 11 attacks, 14
Shilling, Gary, 12, 13, 107, 108
Smartphones, 47
Softbank, 32
Son, Masayoshi, 32, 34, 110
SpaceX, 32, 33, 35
Starlink, 35, 112
step-up basis, 86, 87
super fund, 37
Swensen Portfolio, 28
Swensen, David, 3, 19, 20, 28, 78, 110

T

Taleb, Nassim, 12, 14, 108, 109
tax efficiency, 85, 86, 90
tax-free, 84, 86, 87
technology, 31, 32, 33, 34, 35, 36, 37, 43, 46, 47, 49, 52, 53, 54, 91, 94, 95, 96, 128
TECL, 52, 53, 54

Tesla, 32, 33, 35, 95, 112
The matrix, 36
Tulip Mania, 13

U

U.S. stocks, 4, 61
Unconventional Success, 19, 78, 110

V

Vanguard, 3, 58, 77, 78, 114
video streaming, 47
Vision Fund, 32, 34, 111
Vision Fund 2, 34, 111
VTI, VEA, VWO, VNQ, IEF, TIP, 20

W

Wall Street, x, 2, 12, 37, 64, 66

X

XLK, 52, 53

Notes

_____

_____

_____

_____

_____

_____

_____

_____

_____

_____

_____

_____

_____

Notes

About the Author

David Kreinces is the founder and chief investment officer of ETF Portfolio Management (ETF PM) and the direct manager of ETF PM's separate accounts. Kreinces is also the co-host of the *Investable Benchmark Update (IBU)* podcast, and an ETF judge on the YouTube  webseries *ETF Battles*, sharing his research and market insights.

David's favorite areas of interest include rules-based investing, technology, artificial intelligence, robotics, space exploration, wellness, physical conditioning, and gardening. David's loving family, friends, and numerous pets, based in Southern California, New York, Georgia, and Florida, all help to keep him thankful and grounded.

Made in USA - North Chelmsford, MA
1229079_9781736371008
01.22.2021 1517